CW01558369

Short Stories to Insp.. .. ..ience...

Draw up a Chair...

Compiled and edited by
Elizabeth Medler

Short Stories to Inspire and Experience...

Draw up a Chair...

Sharing stories is a way of increasing our collective wealth. These stories and accompanying exercises will help you to relish the joy of living.

Compiled and edited by
Elizabeth Medler

"It has been said that next to hunger and thirst, our most basic human need is for storytelling."

Khalil Gibran

St Ursin Press

First published in Great Britain in 2018
by St Ursin Press, 3 Broadfield Court,
1-3 Broadfield Road, Folkestone, Kent CT20 2JT, UK

We gratefully acknowledge the financial support of the
Pelegrin Trust in the publication of this book.

Cover design: 'Lotus Rising' by J L Walker © 2018

Set in Garamond 11.5

ISBN 978-0-9955730-3-1

St Ursin Press is an imprint of Trencavel Press
www.trencavel.co.uk/St Ursin.html

For my parents

Acknowledgements

I would like to thank all those who contributed to this book and those who supported it through their love and generosity of spirit.

Contents

Introduction — 1
About the contributors — 6

PART ONE

Angelic Intervention

1. Elizabeth Medler
   The Sweetness of Friendship — 14

2. Julia Shepherd
   Our Guardian Angels Step In   — 18

3. Anna Jeffery
   A Rainbow of Angels — 21

4. Mary Meads
   An Inner Prompting — 24

5. Mary Spain
   A Small Panther on an Upturned Suitcase — 27

PART TWO

What Goes Around Comes Around

6. Philip Pegler
    The Saving Grace of Mischief — 30

7. Arthur Farndell
    Dad's Micrometer — 35

PART THREE

'Chance' Meetings

8. Raymond Payne
    An Angelic Trilogy — 42

9. Elizabeth Medler
    The 'Angel' on the London Underground — 46

10. David Beckwith
    Changing Direction — 50

11. Terry Parris
    God Helps Those Who Help Themselves — 53

12. Meg Bentley
    The Cat on the Bus — 55

13. Ruth Yendell
    The Loving Arms of Providence — 57

PART FOUR

Insights

14. Jane Pittsinger
    How 'El Nino' Synchronously Uprooted my Life and Showed
    me Compassion — 62

15. David Millican
    A Premonition or Just a Dream? — 65

16. Jennifer Dunkley
    Mrs Emsley and the Tea Leaves — 68

17. Paul A Janke
    My Epiphany — 70

18. Josephine Chia
    Chant Your Way Out Of Distress — 74

19. Rose McCray
    My Hip Journey — 77

20. Michael Lewin
    Questions and Answers — Sitting and Waiting Respectfully — 81

21. Jan Walker
    Awakening to my Creative Heart — 83

Introduction

Let's Share our Stories

'We must be willing to let go of the life we planned so as to have the life that is waiting for us.'

Joseph Campbell

Joining up the Dots

These short stories show that in times of great need, we are supported. This support comes in many ways — through mentors, family, friends, strangers and sometimes from unseen Guardian Angels. These radiant beings drop shining pearls into the pool of our minds, prompting us to act or refrain from acting. Sometimes we are guided to say or do things which may seem illogical at the time but, with hindsight, prove to be just the right thing. Again we may have been mulling over a thorny problem for some time when suddenly we begin to see the glimmer of a solution.

Many of us have experienced synchronistic incidents throughout our lives. Always they reveal an underlying Order and serve to remind us of Hamlet's famous words: 'There are more things in heaven and earth, Horatio, than are dreamt of in your philosophy.' These incidents stretch out in multiple forms — from the falling open of a book at a relevant page — to themes in conversations and music, to so called 'chance' meetings. All serve to remind us that in truth we are not alone and that in some mysterious way, all of life is one; every aspect being interrelated with every other aspect in one vast web of relationships.

Introduction

To the lover of wisdom the whole of creation is a living Symbol of the invisible Reality throbbing behind each atom, each blade of grass, each creature and each human being. To others, still yet asleep, there are only 'things' with no innate meaning, order or pattern. The poet Elizabeth Barrett Browning encapsulates this well in her poem 'Aurora Leigh':

Earth's crammed with heaven,
And every common bush afire with God;
But only he who sees, takes off his shoes,
The rest sit round it and pluck blackberries...

Just what is this mysterious Order that lies within and behind creation? We are each King Arthur on a voyage of discovery... it is for us to seek and to find and as we find, we add our own share to the corpus of human knowledge and wisdom.

Mostly we see through a glass darkly, catching glimpses of the Truth, noting them and moving on to the next. We shall never get to the point where we have it all tied-up and neatly boxed as that would imply that Truth is finite. Paradoxically, although the journey is ours, we need guides to shine light on our paths. These can be human mentors, venerable souls from ancient wisdom traditions, and our own Guardian Angel. The light they bring to bear may reveal connections or 'ladders' which expedite our journeys and likewise 'snakes' which may lead us away from the Path of Truth. However, if we 'fall down' a snake we can be sure that a ladder will be close by!

In the course of our journeys we become aware that we are not alone, but assisted — often in hidden ways — to attain our full potential. It is entirely up to us as to whether we are willing to accept assistance from the 'helping hands' surrounding us, but we can only do so if we admit that they are present. If we refuse to recognise them, we block out the light and seem to find ourselves alone. As the stories you will read shortly demonstrate, we are far from alone.

There is another kind of 'alone' — an entirely different one. The great German mystic, Meister Eckhart, alluded to this when he suggested that Jesus ejected the money changers from the temple so that the 'Deep' transcendent (the Divine) could hear Itself in the 'Deep' imminent in creation. Invariably our energies are so dissipated that we can no longer hear the sound of our own inner Voice. It isn't until we calm down and draw to the silent centre of ourselves that we begin to discern the pattern and Order behind creation. Centering brings us back into peaceful alignment so that those aspects of ourselves which have become jumbled and disjointed move back to their rightful places and therefore into right relationship with the psyche as a whole. With this comes coherence and once again we are able to make sense of the world. Often, though, things in our lives do not seem to 'stack up' and it can sometimes be many years before we begin to discern any kind of pattern or order. From this we can see the importance of acceptance and the virtue of faith which allow us to trust that there is a process and a 'Plan'. Unseen visitors and apparent coincidences act as another means to re-align us and remind us that there is a meaning and order behind everything and a 'purpose to everything under the Sun'.

Changelessness and Change

Sound is born from silence and returns to it. Movement is born from stillness and returns to it. Change is born from changelessness and returns to it. This is the path of life. Our understanding of life too often moves from what we are told is true, to exploration — which may involve a rejection of what we are told — to tried and tested experience where we come to see that what we were told is in fact true or not. As that wise soul, Socrates, knew ... once truth is educed from the mind, it has a self-confirmatory aspect. Indeed, each of the stories that follow has a ring of truth about it and this is because the writer is in no doubt as to what happened and how hidden hands supported them.

The perennial or ancient wisdom confirms the changeless nature of real Ideas: a hierarchy of realities which range from absolutely universal Ideas, like Unity, Goodness, Truth and Beauty to the more relative ideas of individual things. The absolute Ideas are ideals also as they represent what we aspire to and lived experience. They are the changeless sources of all change and the powerhouses behind all existence. Once we touch these eternal verities they take us with them and our lives become filled with their power and our minds become open to the plethora of connections all around us.

We become familiar with change as soon as we are born and yet we only know it because of the changeless. As we become more engaged with mundane life, we tend to lose ourselves in the grip of time and the bliss of the changeless recedes. How can we re-enter that blissful unity and regain perspective again?

Fortunately, in the 21st Century, meditation and mindfulness have experienced something of a renaissance. Prayer, meditation, contemplation and ritual describe a path of liberation which far from being escapism, enable us to be considerably more practical and able to deal with the 'nuts and bolts' of daily existence. These sacred practices also serve to slow us down so that we can begin to notice and to 'read' the language of the Cosmos and the connections all around us. As we do this we not only start to discern the workings of Providence but we learn to co-operate with it. Instead of baulking against what comes to us, we embrace it.

Providence could be described as the All-Seeing 'Eye' which has the Absolute Overview. As Divine Justice, Providence dispenses what is right and good to everything and everyone. In the world we see this as Fate — the cosmic 'Knitter', knitting effects to their causes and connecting one thing to another. It seems to me that as we grow in awareness we can become part of the Providential process, facilitating connections of all kinds and being fully alive to possibilities.

Sharing stories

I feel it is important to share our stories because this not only deepens our own reflections and brings light to bear on the cosmic Order, but it has a creative dynamism all of its own. Plato spoke about friends in conversation 'growing up' fair children between them. By sharing our stories we do indeed nourish each other's ideas (our children) so they become strong, well formed, illuminating and forces for good in the world. By bearing witness to the stories of others, we add our own consciousness to them (our own light) and the whole experience becomes enriched.

Introduction

At the end of each story there is a 'pause' point which serves as an exercise in Mindfulness. This will allow you to reflect on some of the lessons it contains and to really make it your own. You may find other aspects which are particularly meaningful and hopefully you can use these to make the story less of an external reading, and more of an inner experience. My heartfelt wish is that you enjoy these stories.

Please write and share your stories with me. I would love to hear from you! lillibet7@icloud.com

About the Contributors

David Beckwith

David spent his childhood and teenage years in the village of Kingswood in Surrey.

Meg Bentley

Meg spent many years teaching children and then used her long held interest in spirituality and creative arts to work with adults.
His work as a surveyor was followed by many years working for a Civil Engineering Consultancy in London, Birmingham and Melbourne. During these years of working in cities David never lost his love for the peace and beauty of the countryside. This love, and gradual spiritual awareness, have been the driving forces in the many changes of directions that have occurred in his life over the years.

Josephine Chia

Josephine is a published author and lived in the UK for many years but now lives in Singapore. In 1992 her short story, 'Tropical Fever' was short-listed for the UK Ian St James Awards. Her memoirs about life in a small village in colonial Singapore, *Kampong Spirit — Gotong Royong: Life in Potong Pasir, 1855 to 1965*, won the Singapore Literature Prize in 2014. This was followed by a sequel, *Goodbye My Kampong, Potong Pasir 1966 to 1975*. Her first Young Adult novel, *Big Tree in a Small Pot*, has just been published. This will be followed by *Growing Up in Kampong Potong Pasir*

— a children's version of her books about her kampong (village). This is expected to be launched in September 2018.

Jennifer Dunkley

Jennifer is a retired Occupational Therapist. Her interest in Philosophy has led to her running Philosophy groups for the U3A and the local WI over the past seventeen years.

Arthur Farndell

After graduating in Modern Languages from Cambridge University, Arthur embarked upon a teaching career in both private and public sectors. His interest in languages led him to join others who were engaged on a project to translate from Latin the twelve volumes of letters written by the fifteenth-century philosopher-priest Marsilio Ficino. After more than forty years, ten of these volumes have been published. Today Arthur directs the Project and collaborates with others in Europe and Australia. He speaks internationally and runs inspiring study courses based on the work of Ficino. His work also includes the translation of five volumes of Ficino's commentaries to the Platonic dialogues.

Arthur has long been attracted by the Sanskrit language, in which he tutored for many years and led courses. He has produced *A Mahābhārata Companion*, which is a guide to the world's longest poem.

Paul A Janke

For over twenty years Paul has used Homoeopathy, spiritual mentoring and a variety of other healing modalities to help people rediscover their wholeness. Originally trained as a company accountant, today Paul understands the power of change and transformation and facilitates this process in others, enabling them to follow their own bliss.

Contributors

Anna Jeffery

Anna lives in Surrey with her husband Michael. She has a background in the health service, school and Church administration. In 1992 she launched Cultural Country Retreats, a national network of retreats 'with a difference', primarily for those on the fringe of the Church who were seeking a meaningful spiritual dimension to their lives. The retreats were successful and ran for many years; they are currently being restructured. Anna is also a published author and has written three books — 'Five Gold Rings', 'Symphony of Life' and 'The Gift'.

Michael Lewin

Michael has served as a Trustee of the Buddhist Hospice Trust, a Committee Member of the Lifestyle Movement and a Member of the Gandhi Foundation. He spent two years living in community, in a Franciscan Friary. He has spent the last twenty-five years teaching and supporting a variety of different groups: young offenders, young unemployed people, children at risk, children with special needs, adults with learning difficulties and adults with mental health needs. Michael holds a BA Degree in Psychology and an MA Degree in Fine Art.

Rose McCray

Rose is an experienced complementary therapist working from home and as a volunteer at a local hospice. She is also an active grandmother, walker, cook and reads widely. She is keen to encourage 'alternative' thinking in health, education and daily life.

Mary Meads

Mary has enjoyed her involvement with the Church over the years and carries her aspirations into the vital work she does for charity with people from many different backgrounds. She believes that she has received far more than she has given.

Contributors

Elizabeth Medler

Elizabeth was Editor of *New Vision* (formerly *The Science of Thought Review*) for some sixteen years. During that time she initiated and ran a varied programme of events. She continues to enjoy writing and runs discussion groups and meditation classes from home.

David Millican

David was born in Cumbria, but now lives on the coast in East Kent with his wife, Ann. He has a background in education, and has worked in South America, the Basque Country and at several colleges and universities within the UK. His pursuit of spiritual Truth has led him to learn and practise a wide range of meditation techniques from different religious and philosophical systems in the world, and to study the universal ideas embodied in the writings of the great teachers of the Perennial Wisdom.

Terry Parris

Throughout her life Terry has worn different 'hats'. In the 1950s she was a broadcaster and actress. Subsequently she became a teacher of English as a foreign language and taught yoga. She is a published author. Terry was a full time tender carer for her husband with whom she had a brood of gifted children, among whom is an artist, an MP and Radio 4 commentator and a political activist who has successfully helped to ban bull fighting in Catalunya. Terry lives in a pretty little farm-house in the foothills of the Pyrenees not far from Barcelona.

Raymond Payne

Raymond has been a student of philosophy — that is the pursuit of the love of wisdom — all his adult life. He is a member of the School of Economic Science (a school of practical philosophy) based in London. For the last seven years he has been the leader of one of its Branch Schools, the Wessex School of Philosophy, which provides classes on practical philosophy in a number of venues across central southern England.

Contributors

Philip Pegler

Born into a literary family near London in 1947, Philip was educated at Harrow School and trained as a journalist on a local newspaper before becoming an antiquarian bookseller. At the age of twenty-two, he gave up his job to travel to India in quest of Truth. His profoundly memorable experiences there have inspired and informed a life dedicated to spiritual inquiry ever since. Philip has been writing about spirituality for over forty years and has two biographies to his credit. He is married to Wendy and they live on the South Downs in West Sussex.

Jane Pittsinger

Jane was born and grew up in Sri Lanka on a tea estate. She went to boarding school in England from the age of ten and later studied to become a physiotherapist in London enabling her to travel and work in other countries. While working in Colombia, South America, she met her American husband and settled with him in the San Francisco Bay area in the 1980s. She practises the Rosen Method which is a mind/body therapeutic method. She has always had an interest in what is universal to all human beings throughout all cultures and ages and how soul potential can be unfolded.

Julia Shepherd

Julia trained as a healer at the College of Psychic Studies. She is a tutor, supervisor and examiner of healing at both the College of Psychic Studies and the School of Intuition and Healing. Julia is a Reiki Master and teacher.

Mary Spain

Mary is a gifted poet and teacher. She lives in London with her beautiful cat, Chloe. Together they work for the charity 'Pets As Therapy'. Mary writes her own very vital and insightful blog spot: www.lettersfromlondon19blogspot.co.uk

Contributors

Jan Walker

Jan has enjoyed writing for as long as long as she can remember. Today she works from her mountain home in California. Her articles have been published both in the USA and UK. She is also a gifted painter and teaches Chinese brush painting. She is currently writing a novel of historical fiction set in ancient China.

Ruth Yendell

Ruth was born into a Quaker family in 1940. Throughout her early years she found her purpose in life in her love of music, and specifically the violin. While coming to the end of her musical studies in London, her hunger for God led her finally to the Roman Catholic Church, into which she was received aged 21. Two marvellously enriching, but in the end abortive, attempts to become a nun followed several years later. After the collapse of the second, she came to accept that both attempts had served an essential, but temporary, purpose in the growth and deepening of her faith. She is now happy keeping up her prayer life and pursuing musical and artistic interests.

Part One

~ 'Angelic' intervention ~

'For he shall give his angels charge over thee,
to keep thee in all thy ways. They shall bear
thee up in their hands, lest thou dash thy
foot against a stone.'

Psalm 91: 11-12

Elizabeth's story
Julia's story
Anna's story
Mary's story
Mary's story

Elizabeth Medler

The Sweetness of Friendship

Ted Mappley was a rare kind of man — an adventurer, mine disposal officer, diver, fisherman, Sea captain, truck driver, countryman.

It was Wednesday 22 May 2013, I had been very busy at work and cycled home fairly slowly. After preparing supper and relaxing, my mind suddenly turned to my friend, Ted Mappley, who had moved into a nursing home at the end of April.

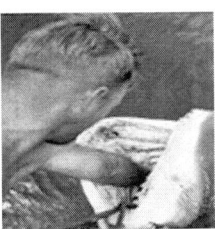

Ted handling a shark

Ted — Mine Disposal Officer, Royal Navy

Ted was truly an exceptional human being. He lived in a small bungalow at the end of my road and owned the orchard close by. I had met Ted in 2003 when I moved to the area and on occasions I helped him in the orchard. Despite being well into his 80s, he managed to maintain the orchard, his home and his garden. My usual job was to cut the ivy at the root of each tree, but it was a thankless task as the trees were old and gnarled and each year the ivy seemed to make massive inroads. Then there were bonfires and apple collecting. Ted was a countryman and showed me how to gather up the apples under each tree so that birds overwintering could feast on them.

He was strict about his tools and taught me to gather them up together rather than leave them dotted around the orchard.

Ted wasn't just a 'whizz' outside, he was an accomplished cook, making huge quantities of marmalade, relish and excellent meals.

Occasionally, he would become ill and at one point a bed had to be moved into his front room as one of his legs had become ulcerated and needed to be kept elevated. Moving the bed from his bedroom to the front room is a story all of its own! His niece (Liz) and I struggled to get the bed out, but we could not... in the end Liz was obliged to take the door off its hinges, which took some doing! Despite this passing illness Ted continued his outdoor life, keeping his tools always well sharpened and arranged neatly in his shed.

Over the years, he was a marvellous 'listening ear' and gave me wonderful advice when I needed it. Despite being of the World War II generation (Ted was a mine disposal officer — removing and making safe mines from the sea), he was in many respects a timeless individual.

During his work as a diver he naturally met many other divers and even knew the secret of the mystery of Lionel Crabb ('Buster' Crabb) — a Royal Navy frogman who vanished on 19 April 1956 during a mission around a Soviet cruiser docked at Portsmouth. I never pressed Ted about this as it was clearly something close to his heart.

Ted wasn't typically English. He travelled to many parts of the world and had lived on a boat he refurbished which he sailed through the Bay of Biscay to Alicante, living there moored in the harbour. Subsequently he lived with his first wife of thirteen years (Susie) in a villa north of Alicante. Then for a period he lived on a boat moored on the Canal du Midi in Southern France. There he befriended Henri and Suzette. Henri was similarly practical and Suzette was a good cook.

Ted could really turn his hand to anything — skin animals, ride horses, drive trucks, fish (there is a photo of him as a young man with his hand in the jaws of a shark).

Ted and I would often sit in his conservatory and he would point out all the birds in the garden — he knew their names and when they were likely to fly in. He would sit back in his chair quietly and listen to my news. If it was help I needed, he would listen wisely and only comment after a few seconds silence. He would share with me his own life experience. Sometimes, these included ghost stories! He was a believer in life after death and reincarnation.

In 1997 Ted married the love of his life, Mary. They lived quietly together in the little bungalow. Sadly though, after only seven years, Mary contracted throat cancer. Ted nursed her bravely through this very difficult illness but she died eighteen months later. Mary remained in Ted's heart, but he was an immensely resourceful and practical individual and this enabled him to continue to live a very full life. One of his greatest gifts was the ability to enjoy his own company but he was not a loner and relished company. On a number of occasions he invited me over, together with his lovely niece, Liz and we enjoyed a meal together.

Returning now to the evening of the 22nd May... There arose within me a strong urge to go and see Ted. I glanced at my watch and realised it was 8.30pm — too late to visit. I did my best to ignore the inner prompting by phoning a friend. I chatted to her for some fifteen minutes but still the feeling would not leave me. Finally, I could resist no longer, jumping on to my bike I cycled down to the home and walked up the stairs to Ted's bedroom. As I entered the room I saw Ted on the bed. His mouth was open and it became immediately evident that he had passed on. I soon found one of the staff who initially seemed unconcerned as someone had spoken to him recently. They came with me to the bedroom and indeed confirmed that Ted had died. Initially, whilst they checked, they asked me to remain outside but then they allowed me into the room on my own. I shut the door and my first words were: 'Ted, well done for getting out of your old body' and then I said the Lord's Prayer. I was genuinely pleased for Ted that he had shuffled off what is a very mortal coil. He was so young and vital. It was time for him to leave.

It was such a blessing to be the first person to see Ted after his departure and I am convinced he 'called' me. He was, and remains, a true friend and I shall never forget him.

Ted on horseback in the USA

 *Pause for thought...*

What does true friendship mean to you? Today, let's value the friends we have and be ready to meet new friends.

Julia Shepherd

Our Guardian Angels Step In

It is said that we each have a guardian angel. In Julia's case, her angel stepped in to avert an accident which might have had very serious consequences.

It was Spring 2003 and my daughter Freya was nearly three years old when she and I went to visit an old friend, taking the London tube from our home in Ealing, to Fulham where my friend lived.

As usual, we were rushing to catch the tube, having been held up by goodness knows what, and arrived at the station ticket barriers just as the train was pulling into the platform. I managed to negotiate the ticket machines and Freya and I hurried to the steps leading to the platform. Freya was excited to be going on the tube and she was walking as fast as she could so as to catch the train.

I took her little hand and we began to rush down the flight of stone stairs towards the train which had by now stopped at the platform. I recall that my only focus was to catch the train. Rather irresponsibly, I must have been carelessly placing my feet on each step, practically pulling Freya along and she was about one step higher than me on those industrial stairs.

Suddenly, I found myself falling, firstly downwards and then, as I tried to save myself, I lurched towards Freya who was still at my side and slightly above me. In an attempt to steady myself, I took a big, heavy step towards a stair. I can still see in my mind's eye my large adult foot heading for the unforgiving, stone stair, just as Freya was about to place her little foot in the same place. In a split second, Freya's foot found the step and in my unbalanced state, there was nothing I could do to stop my foot slamming onto hers and undoubtedly crushing her foot and ankle into the right-angle of the stone rise of the stair.

Panic and a sense of horror overwhelmed me, when suddenly, inexplicably, I found my foot was being prevented from coming into contact with Freya's foot by some sort of force. It was as if my foot was being held, just above hers, hovering, with what felt like a cushion underneath it so it was unable to slam onto the stair.

Then, instantly, we were on the train. Again, it was as if a force had carried us onto that tube.

Sitting on the train, shocked and quite frankly, amazed at what had happened, I tried to make sense of the events which had unfolded in seconds. Fortunately, Freya was unaffected and chatted happily as the tube weaved its way through West London.

I sat and centred myself and it became obvious to me that we had been blessed with some spiritual intervention of some sort. I feel most strongly that it was either my or Freya's Guardian Angel (or maybe both), who had worked to stop me falling onto Freya's foot and ankle and seriously injuring her. The same helpers had carried us onto the train that day.

Every time I think about the incident, I feel a grip of fear as to what damage I could have done to my daughter's little foot and ankle, albeit accidentally. Crushed into a stone stair, she may not have walked properly for ages, if at all. The consequences are too awful to contemplate.

As it turned out, Freya is very sporty and is a beautiful ballet dancer. She has passed all her grades and has done some of the vocational training too, even once auditioning for the Royal Ballet School.

Over the years, every time I saw Freya dance, I would think of what happened that day and thank, most humbly, whatever angel, guide or other being of Light that was with us that day.

Also, even now, when I feel alone or unsupported, I take strength from that Presence and remind myself that I am neither alone or unsupported. Wonderfully, I know from this experience that neither is Freya.

 *Pause for thought...*

Draw close to your Guardian Angel today and ask for guidance to meet the blessings and challenges of the day.

Anna Jeffery

A Rainbow of Angels

Anna's story recounts the appearance of several angels each of whom was a harbinger of glad tidings in her life.

"*Once upon a time...*" as all good stories begin ... and a long time ago I had a dream. That dream began with sounds of a celestial choir singing:

"From out of eternity each new day doth dawn ... and back to eternity at night doth return..."

As it faded, I saw an angel — a deep blue angel — gliding silently over to where I was sitting — and she began telling me how my Christian faith would develop during my lifetime on Earth.

It would begin, she said, through a fellow student in the Sixth form who would take me aside and proceed to explain the importance of 'becoming a Christian' as she would put it. As this would seem to meet an unspoken need, I would thus embark on my Christian journey. However some years later I would start 'back-sliding'. I would stop going to church and would no longer feel at ease with what I perceived to be a restrictive approach to life. I would wrestle with guilt, confusion and a sense of sin. This she foretold would result in a virtual spiritual breakdown.

Gradually this blue angel faded away and after a time, as I sat there musing on what she had said, the celestial choir sang again and with the fading music a second angel appeared — this time robed in a beautiful leaf green — who continued the prediction of how my faith would develop. This time it would be through meeting a monk who would recognise the hugely confused spiritual state in which I would find myself. He would progress my spiritual life even further by helping me to re-inform my belief system, convincing me that true spirituality could be far wider, deeper and broader than anything I had experienced up until then. He would teach me that as human beings we were on a spiritual journey leading to true fulfilment. We should aim, he would say, to be the very best that we can be with a deep conviction and assurance underpinning everything we do. And so, greatly uplifted by a newly invigorated prayer life, I would begin to live more fully again.

Eventually this angel too faded and after another verse from the celestial choir, a third angel appeared in a beautiful rosy hue. This angel predicted that while working at a hospital, I would meet someone with a razor sharp mind and a voice like thunder who would embark on a discourse about belief and spirituality. I would recognise immediately the voice of rare authority — the voice in fact, of a mystic. And thus my faith would emerge, greatly strengthened by these latter two angels. I would be uplifted by a newly invigorated prayer life, and would begin to be fully alive again instead of burdened with the negativity of the former evangelical approach. At which point, a fourth angel appeared — this time robed in deep purple but only after that familiar verse from the celestial choir. This angel would affect my life very deeply as he imparted the teachings of a gifted philosopher.

These predictions preceded the appearance of a fifth angel, in pure white robes and after more celestial music, he foretold essential facts about my spiritual life explaining that my first spiritual project — Cultural Country Retreats — 'would be a rich blessing to many'.

Realising now that this whole visitation of angels in various hues, were forming the most beautiful rainbow — each one with an incredible prediction — I was excited to see how many more there might be. While I was musing on this, that celestial choir sang out again and there in front of me, was my sixth angel, robed in purest gold — conveying the deepest of spiritual insights so far, including the fact that:

A Life without Meaning

A Life without Values

A Life without Hope

would make life a real struggle but if I could identify:

 A Purpose to live for

 A Self to Live with

 A Faith to Live by

life would be wonderfully fulfilling.

And so it was that no less than six angels — forming that amazing rainbow — foretold how my spiritual life would develop.

It is strange how in the angelic realms, time telescopes in such a way that years pass in an instant... thus a span of what must have been years in Earth time, passed in what must have been minutes in the realm of angels.

The memory of this dream, far more meaningful than any other dream — either before or since — has remained with me until this day.

 *Pause for thought...*

As a new day dawns, ask your guardian angel to be with you and guide you. At the end of the day recount, briefly, all that you have done and give thanks for it. If you have done something which jars your conscience, put it right the next day or send a prayer after it.

Mary Meads

An Inner Prompting

Mary's life changed dramatically when she received an inner prompting to make contact with people she had not seen for years.

In the Summer of 1962 I attended a meditation and discussion meeting in Crondace Road, Fulham, led by a lady called Constance Peters. We reflected on the rule of 'obeying the Holy Spirit'. I recall Constance saying that it was very important for us to have times of complete quiet, to be still and know that God is our God and to be receptive to the Holy Spirit.

The idea took hold of me. Yes, I would try it, particularly as at that time my little world had completely collapsed. I had come through years of unhappiness until my spirit was almost broken and I felt a great need to rebuild and, just like the phoenix, to rise again...

Home I went and, as soon as possible, set aside an evening to have this time of silence and receptivity. I put myself in a relaxed position, wiped, as it were, the slate of my mind clean of all thoughts, wishes and desires and became completely at peace with myself. As I settled down, a thunderstorm began, but this did not destroy my peace and serenity. During this relaxing time a strange thing happened ... a voice seemed to say, 'Ring the Middleton's'. My immediate response was to ignore this, thinking that perhaps it was my imagination at work, and yet the gentle prompting persisted. You see, I had not seen the Middleton's for four years, nor had I kept in touch with them or they with me. I had met them on holiday and they were just two of a very happy group of thirty or forty people.

I recalled Constance's words: 'If a prompting comes, do not delay but obey immediately.' It was not easy to obey as I had no idea of the Middleton's telephone number or address. However, I remembered the name of their town so I searched the directory which would give me that. I found the name, but there were four people of that name in the town. Which was it? Then I recalled that Mrs Middleton had told me she lived on a hilltop, so I looked for an address which might give me a clue to this. Ah! There was one which sounded hopeful, so I took the plunge and picked up the 'phone.

A man answered my call, his voice soft and kindly, and I said, '*Are you the gentleman who took a holiday to Madrid four years ago with the Kenilworth party?*' '*Yes, indeed I am*,' he said. '*Well, I didn't expect to find you in, but was convinced you might be in sunny Spain or Italy! You don't know who I am, do you?*' No, he didn't, but when I gave him my name he said: '*Well, I was thinking of you only yesterday!*'

'*How is your wife?*' I enquired. There was a hollow silence, then he told me she had died some months earlier. I expressed my sympathy and he then enquired where I was and what I was doing. I briefly explained that my life had changed dramatically and a chapter of my life was over, but on a positive note, I was starting another life. I had a job which drew upon me in a positive way and having broken down old patterns, I was living an entirely new life.

Mike Middleton said he would like to see me again. A week later we met and much to my great surprise, he proposed to me. I said he would have to be very patient for my answer as I needed to be one hundred percent sure, for his sake as well as mine. He was considerably older than I was and, at the time, that seemed to be a barrier. Since then I have realised that barriers can be blessings!

Nineteen months later we were married and I thank God daily for all the abundant happiness that we shared together.

To those in distress I would say: Be patient, the things of the Spirit work out. Do not fret or worry. Keep your thoughts positive and the Sun will shine again for you. Believe in this truly. Out of your present situation there may be lessons to be learned and perhaps you cannot go forward until the blockage (whatever it may be) has been removed. Respect your body. Don't overtax it, keep it a pure channel for God's love to flow in and through you.

Daily, if at all possible, do some small kindness or act of love for another.

Accept whatever life brings. Offer yourself and it to God and eventually happiness and peace of mind will come.

 *Pause for thought...*

Today, can we be patient and allow things to unfold in their own time without unwise intervention?

Mary Spain

A Small Panther on an Upturned Suitcase

This story shows how tokens of consolation can materialise, almost out of thin air, from those who love us.

Have you ever had a totally inexplicable experience... an experience which, rather than leaving you confused, gave you instead a wonderful sense of love and support? This happened to me a few years ago with the unexpected arrival of a small panther.

I was an only child and my mother and I were very close. When she was in her mid-eighties she left her home in Somerset and, together with Sophie, our Siamese cat, came to live with me in London. The three of us formed a happy, loving household.

Mother died six years later. Less than two months after her death, Sophie, then aged twenty, also died. My family, which hadn't been large to start with, had shrunk dramatically from three to one — all in a matter of weeks.

My mother's room, the room in which she died, became my book-room, as I'm sure she would have wanted. Her furniture was given away and, in its place, I brought in bookshelves, a desk, a computer, a television and an easy chair. Soon, all that remained of my mother's possessions was the suitcase of clothing which stood below the window waiting to be collected by Oxfam.

It was at this juncture, shortly after Sophie's death, that I was sitting one evening watching television. Behind me was the closed window below which was the suitcase of clothing. Sitting there, I suddenly felt chilly, it was as though there was a draught. Getting to my feet, I went round to the back of the chair to check on the window. It was firmly shut. About to return to my original position, I chanced to look down... and it was then that I received a considerable shock.

There, sitting on the upturned suitcase, was a very small panther. It was no more than two inches long, made in all probability of plastic. Crouching happily on the suitcase, it looked completely at home.

I stared at it in amazement. This was something I'd never seen before. My thoughts raced... where on earth had it come from? No children had been in the room since mother had died, and mother had most definitely never had such a thing as a small, plastic panther. It couldn't have come through the window of a third floor flat. Not only that, being mid-winter, the window had been shut for quite a while. The suitcase had been placed behind the chair only a few days previously... so, where on earth, or heaven, had the panther come from?

I fully expected the small figure to dematerialise before my eyes, but it didn't. Accepting its reality, I picked it up. It was beautifully made and very tangible. Perplexed, but grateful, I put it in a purse in my handbag, where it has remained ever since.

Where did the panther come from? All I can think is that it was a gift from mother... a 'cat companion' until the arrival of Sophie's successor. How did it come? Well, I'm sure you would agree that there's nothing the angels can't achieve!

 *Pause for thought...*

Today, let's open our minds to the tokens of love all around us.

Part Two

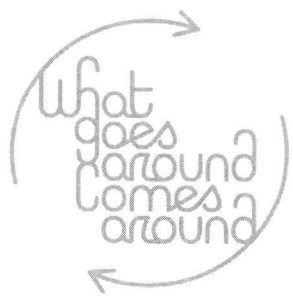

'The idea of karma is that you continually
get the teachings that you need to open
your heart.'

Pema Chodron

Philip's story
Arthur's story

Philip Pegler

The Saving Grace of Mischief

Philip's story shows how what seems to be mistaken, and even foolish, can prove to be a saving grace.

Numerous photos of my mother in our family albums testify to her fetching beauty — and certainly in that respect her good looks and vivacious manner have always been for me a distinct matter of pride. Hardly surprising by virtue of family loyalty, but for me it is a normal response made all the more poignant by the sad fact that she died far too young, aged just fifty-four, after illness in the wake of a catastrophic road accident.

Time heals even the deepest of wounds and I have long got over my loss. Nowadays I derive strength and insight from recollections of her distinctive life and my significant part in it. For example, I value the unusual fact that I was born on my mother's birthday, which every year made that shared day of November 23rd special for us both. We naturally enjoyed a close bond and so she was inclined to forgive quite easily most of my misdeeds. That is just as well considering the tale I am about to relate...

One particular snap, pasted in a scrapbook belonging to my mother, stands out from all the rest, because it is from an actual newspaper cutting. This photo evidently belongs to the glittering period before I was born, when as a fashionable debutante, my mother had recently been presented at court, as was the custom in those more elegant days before the Second World War.

On this occasion, to my modern-day eyes at least, she definitely does not appear at her best. She looks a bit awkward in an unflattering hat set at a jaunty angle and the caption is curious too, hinting at the stiff social attitudes still prevalent in that unstable, inter-war period.

'Modern youth is frighteningly intelligent,' reads the caption in mild alarm as it suggests more than a trace of concern on the part of an older generation struggling to contain the excesses of their offspring. How little has changed down the years in that regard. Precocious and intelligent my mother certainly was, but equally true is the undoubted actuality that she was to impart to all of her three sons the rebellious streak noticed by the London *Evening Standard* in that cutting from around 1932.

I realise in hindsight that when I was an adolescent like her, I was precocious, if not downright inconsiderate and capable on occasions of breathtaking presumption. Take for example the following incident that still prompts in me astonished embarrassment fifty years on.

Like many young men I was keen on fast cars and was always more than pleased to welcome to our home a close school friend, who sported a high-performance Mini-Cooper, which I particularly admired for its rapid acceleration.

One afternoon as we closely inspected its powerful, small engine, my friend suddenly turned to me and his face lit up with enthusiasm as he was seized by a bright idea.

'Why don't we pep-up your mother's car?' he suggested innocently. 'There is a lot we ourselves could do with little outlay. Not many parts would be needed and the work would not take long. We can complete the work right here in your garage. What about it?'

I hesitated uneasily for a moment, as I considered what my mother might say.

'Are you sure you can put the engine properly together again after you have taken it apart?' I asked cautiously.

'Of course,' Tony replied with disarming confidence. 'I have done this sort of thing many times. You have absolutely no need to worry.'

There was another brief moment of distinct hesitation on my part and then I threw caution to the winds and took the plunge.

'All right then,' I said bravely. 'Let's go ahead.'

Without further ado we drove off in the Mini-Cooper to fetch the new piston-head we needed to carry out the overhaul, and upon our return, my friend-turned-mechanic, set to work immediately.

Before long bits of engine lay scattered about the garage floor and what a mess it was, but even so Tony continued to make good progress as the afternoon steadily wore on and my doubts gradually receded. So far so good — and then without warning our luck broke.

Suddenly my mother appeared as if from nowhere at the entrance to the garage.

'What on earth are you doing? What are you doing to my car?' she cried out in outraged disbelief as she surveyed the disordered scene before her.

Mercifully time has blurred the jagged outlines of my memory, but in that moment of crisis one thing was certain. I needed all the tact I could muster as Tony and I endured the full fury of my mother's wrath.

I thoroughly deserved her censure — I can see that clearly now. It is a measure of my youthful disregard you see, that I had totally failed to take into account her most understandable unease regarding anything to do with cars at this point in time. After all, it was barely a year since both my parents had been involved in a head-on collision when another car attempted to overtake a line of lorries on a wet road in Suffolk — and careered at speed into their own vehicle.

My mother sustained multiple cuts to her face when she struck the windscreen and came near to death through loss of blood. Her return to some semblance of normal life after emergency care in hospital had been painfully slow. She was still very much in recovery mode — and our unexpected prank was an unwelcome reminder of her recent trauma.

Perhaps it is just as well that I did not realise how badly her health had been undermined by the shock of this terrible accident. The sad fact remains that she was soon to become struck down by cancer and was to die just two years later.

On that distinctive occasion when we decided to tune-up her car, she actually displayed remarkable restraint. It is a credit to her loving nature that she did calm down from her parental fury before too long. For his part Tony returned without further ado to the urgent task of reassembling the engine. What a relief it was when my mother's car was back in one piece — ready for the road with enhanced power.

That very evening my mother and I went out to her favourite pub — and I took the wheel of her souped-up saloon, keen to show that all was well as I tried out its paces. As we approached our destination, I slowed the car and indicated to turn right into the pub car park as usual. And then out of the corner of my eye, I saw a vehicle coming round the bend ahead — way too far over and heading straight for us.

Instinctively in that unexpected moment of emergency, I swerved to the near side and pressed hard on the accelerator pedal at the same time to complete my turn across the road as quickly as possible. I felt immediately the welcome surge of unaccustomed power as we smartly drove out of the way of the on-coming car and into the safety of the pub car park.

'See — that proves it. I knew a bit of extra speed might be useful in times of trouble,' I proclaimed to my mother with huge gratitude for our escape but mixed, I must admit, with just a bit of self-satisfaction.

I cannot remember what my mother said in reply — but in that precious moment I knew I had been let off the hook and finally forgiven for my misdemeanour.

It is curious when things work out for the best in the end, despite our own failings and lapses of judgement. The mischief for which I had been chiefly responsible had turned out to be a saving grace. It is entirely possible we could never have avoided such an imminent collision if the performance of my mother's car had not been enhanced by my presumption and my friend's considerable mechanical skill.

 *Pause for thought...*

Today be receptive to your inner promptings even when they seem to defy common sense.

Arthur Farndell

Dad's Micrometer

Fred and Bert refused to compromise when it came to the truth. Do we have the strength and moral courage to follow their example in our own lives?

D ad kept a piece of metal in his jacket pocket. Actually, it wasn't right to think of it as a piece of metal, as I discovered when I was a bit older and he was prepared to show it to me. It was a beautiful example of precision craftsmanship. Dad called it his micrometer, which he pronounced *my-KROMM-itta*. He used it at work to check the measurements of the components made in the factory. Dad was called an engineers' inspector. His micrometer was accurate to one thou. He didn't say this word the way the vicar in the village church intoned it. He said it like the beginning of 'thousand'. I learned that it was actually the first syllable of 'thousandth'. A thousandth of an inch! The smallest I could find on my wooden school ruler was an eighth.

As a very young child, I found more comfort in the other pocket. This contained Dad's pipe, tobacco, and Swan Vestas. We didn't see Dad very often. At the outset of World War II the family was evacuated from London. Mum and her three children were sent to a small village in Huntingdonshire, while Dad went to a city in the Midlands where he could find work. So Dad came to see us only two or three times a year. But that gave me the chance to sit on his knee as he filled and lit his pipe prior to telling me stories of three adventurers named Jack, Sam, and Pete.

Dad wasn't well educated. He'd answered the call to arms at the age of 18 in the previous war and then spent four years in the trenches in France. He didn't speak much about those times, at least not in my hearing. All I ever overheard was, 'One moment your mate was there, and the next he was gone, blown to bits by a shell' and 'When the war was over, we were carried shoulder-high around Trafalgar Square.'

I think he made up the stories about Jack, Sam, and Pete. What did it matter? I could settle securely into his lap, enclosed in a cocoon of tobacco smoke and transported into a world of adventure and heroism. Jack was good with a rifle, Sam with a revolver, and Pete with a knife. Dad pulled at his pipe and soon became as relaxed as I was. The three men were always together and they always beat the baddies. Every time Dad came to see us I clambered onto his knee, begging for a story about Jack, Sam, and Pete, and waited contentedly for the pipe ritual to set the scene. And he always obliged. I didn't care that his inventive faculties sometimes wore thin. I just wanted those precious times to go on for ever.

I came to understand that Dad had to pay for his tobacco and that he was beginning to find this expenditure a bit difficult. The solution to the problem and to Dad's anxiety presented itself clearly to my young mind. There were unlimited free supplies of tobacco in the village cow-fields. One Sunday afternoon, while Dad was dozing, I took his pipe with me and searched for the cow-pat that was the closest in colour to the tobacco in Dad's pouch. My tiny fingers and thumb filled the bowl and tamped down the dry brown stuff in the manner that I had witnessed on numerous occasions. My young heart brimmed with pride and joy as I presented the pipe to Dad when he awoke. He was shocked and upset that I had ruined his hopes of enjoying a good smoke. But he didn't scold me. Indeed, he joined in the general laughter after some moments, and the incident went into the family archives, to be brought out and recounted in future years whenever we were reminiscing.

Dad's Micrometer

Dad died during my undergraduate days, and I took the train from Cambridge to attend the funeral. My function was to read a passage from the Bible and give a short eulogy. Dad had never been a great social person, and the mourners numbered no more than twenty. An elderly man sitting by himself in one of the rear pews caught my attention while I was standing at the altar and facing everyone. He was quite well turned out, but it was evident that life had treated him as a punch-bag. Afterwards, as we walked from the chapel to the community centre where the reception was being held, he fell into step beside me and started to talk.

He said his name was Bert. He had known Dad for many years. They had worked together at the same factory, checking the accuracy of components made by the factory. As if to prove his point, he drew from his jacket pocket an object which was instantly recognisable. It was a micrometer. He went on to tell me that he knew things about Dad that hadn't been mentioned at the service. I sent up an instant prayer that this stranger was not going to bring disgrace upon Dad's name. As Bert's tale unfolded, however, it became apparent that my concern was one of those needless anxieties which we so often allow to plague our hearts and minds.

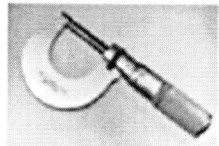

'I'd already been in the factory some years when your Dad arrived from London at the start of the war. By that time, of course, the government had switched us to turning out things for the army. It was quite a big factory and I was in a team of 8 engineers' inspectors. Your Dad made number 9. We knew him as Fred, of course. He was a good worker, but he didn't mix in too well. His mind seemed to be fixed on his family a hundred miles away.'

By this time we had reached the community centre. Mum had made all the refreshments that morning and was now ensuring that everyone got a mug of tea to go with the sandwiches. I found it a comfort to wind my fingers around that fat mug after our walk in the chilly November afternoon. My brother and sister were playing their part by circulating among the other mourners. Bert and I sat at a corner table.

'Well, things ticked over OK until the summer of '43. That's when Steve Dock — the top foreman — called a meeting of the engineers' inspectors. We knew something was wrong because he never called meetings. He told us that profits were sinking rapidly. The situation was serious. "You are the key figures here," he said. "You're turning down too many of the components we make. If you start passing more, we may have a chance of keeping our heads above water." "But we're only following government specifications," said Fred. "Maybe," Steve answered, "but look where it's taken us. From now on I want all of you to start passing components if they are accurate to 2 thou, or even 3." Most of the team looked bewildered, but Fred spoke up without hesitation. "One thou is the government spec. We've got to keep to that." "I agree with Fred," I said. "It could put lives in danger if we allow greater tolerance." The other inspectors kept silent. The foreman turned on Fred and me: "In that case, you two are sacked as from the end of this week. You can pick up your last wages on Friday. The rest of you, do as I say. Meeting closed."

'So there we were, without work. Fred and me decided to stick together. We left the rooms where we lodged. The city had suffered terribly from air raids and there were bombed-out buildings everywhere. We chose one which would act as some sort of dwelling for us. We pooled what cash we had and bought basic tools and equipment. There was one thing we both understood: metal.'

Mum was now coming round with plates of scones that she had baked. She was justifiably proud of her scones.

'Fred and me managed to stay alive by going around the city offering our services. There were always knives to sharpen, pans and kettles to mend, damaged pipes to fix. In the outlying villages and farms there was more work than we could handle. It wasn't top-class engineering, but the money it brought us was enough to keep us alive.'

Mum's friend, Alice, came to top up our mugs from a metal tea-pot so huge that she found it difficult to control the outpour. Bert added three hefty spoonfuls of sugar and stirred thoughtfully. He sipped the hot brew for long minutes before continuing.

'One day early in '44 the front page of the local paper reported that Steve Dock had been sacked and was in some danger of facing prosecution. It seemed that three soldiers had lost their lives as a direct result of the equipment they were using. It didn't take long to trace where that defective equipment was made, and before you could say Jack Robinson, that was that.'

Bert lit a Woodbine and stood up. Suddenly he looked quite frail and wan.

'After the war, things started looking up for us... but that's another story. As for your Dad, I got to know him quite well, of course. He was a good man.' Through smoky breath he added, 'And courageous.'

He put out his hand to shake mine and walked out of the community centre into the dusk of an autumn evening. I never saw him again.

Dad hadn't made a Will. He didn't have much to leave. But Mum said he was insistent that I should have his micrometer. It sits at my bedside, on its worn tan pouch, a constant reminder of goodness and courage.

 *Pause for thought...*

Do we hold our principles dear? Can we speak up today if we need to?

Part Three

~ 'Chance' Meetings ~

'I believe that I am guided by chance encounters. I believe in the miracle of chance encounters.'

Paulo Coelho

Raymond's story
Elizabeth's story
David's story
Terry's story
Meg's story
Ruth's story

Raymond Payne

An Angelic Trilogy

Ring of Truth

Whilst driving to Bournemouth with my wife one evening for a meeting I noticed the petrol gauge was in the red zone and decided to do something about it on the way home. Promptly forgetting to do anything about the petrol situation after the meeting, I found that the car, being starved of fuel, refused to go any further than half way along a busy dual carriageway a long way outside Bournemouth and seemingly in the middle of nowhere!

Self-criticism reigned but that was not going to get the necessary ingredients for the car. I got out, wondering what to do. A car immediately stopped in front of me. A young man got out and instantly recognising the mess I was in said he would go and fetch some fuel and would return in about twenty minutes. I gave him a £10 note and in exchange and as surety for his return he gave me his gold wedding ring and said, "Don't tell my wife!", who fortunately was not with him.

About thirty minutes later I heard a car stop on the other side of the carriageway. The man had returned and, with a petrol can in his hand, he leapt over the central road barrier. He said that he would pour the petrol into the filler cap for me as he was sure I wouldn't wish to spill any on the nice suit I was wearing! My already thankful and good feeling towards him increased even more, and still more when he insisted on giving me the change from the £10 note despite my protestations. He did however take his gold wedding ring back! The young man had the ring of truth about him; he did what he said he would do and by his generosity turned a desperate situation into one of immense gratitude.

The memory of this dream, far more meaningful than any other dream — either before or since — has remained with me until this day.

A Magical Manifestation

Whilst driving on a winding country road on a very windy winter's day, I suddenly had to swerve to avoid crashing into some very large branches that were lying part way across my side of the road and just beyond a bend. On returning an hour later I noticed they were still there and drove past them. A moment's thought said someone else will move them followed immediately by, "It's the Council's job to do it and I will let them know about it. But who will I tell and when will they be there, if ever?"

Swayed by common sense I turned the car around and parked beyond the fallen branches. I thought it would be easy to pull them off the road but as soon as I did and let go of them, they annoyingly swung back onto the road! I tried again with the same result. I tried breaking them and a few twigs came off but nothing more. These branches were resisting all human effort and clung steadfastly to the road!

Another car stopped and a man got out to help. Between us surely we would succeed against this natural opposition. But we couldn't. By now we had quite an audience of car-bound watchers queuing on both sides of the road. I thought and said, "We need a saw", which were the only words I spoke to the man. He said nothing and carried on pulling and tugging. Like me, he didn't have the tool we needed.

A very large skip lorry stopped. The driver got out and disappeared round the other side of his cab. As if by magic and as though answering a prayer, he re-appeared with a saw in his hand. He came over and cut the offending branches from their trunk. The other man and I threw the branches as far as we could on to the roadside verge. The lorry driver got back into his cab and drove off. The man got into his car and drove off. All the stopped cars drove off. I got into my car and drove off. No words passed between any of us except my plea for a saw!

If only life could proceed with such few words and the right tools and action manifest when needed, how magical this would be (and perhaps is.)

A Miracle?

Late one Friday afternoon in mid-summer I was looking forward to going home after a long and difficult week in the office. The 'Friday feeling' was buoyant inside of me. I cleared my desk and headed into the car park. As I looked at my car the Friday feeling suddenly became deflated — one of the front tyres was experiencing the same feeling! I wouldn't be going home just yet!

The car looked drivable for a short distance. The image of a nearby tyre-fitting garage came to mind, if I could just remember where exactly it was. I drove slowly along the back streets hoping to find a new tyre. I recognised the right road and the right building but to my great disappointment the building was not only closed but had also been transformed into some sort of warehouse; there was no tyre in sight!

Feeling somewhat disconsolate, I looked for a suitable place to park the car and change the wheel. Just before turning onto a main road, I found the ideal spot and parked the car. Within an instant another car stopped nearby. A man with his wife and three young children were in the car and I wondered why they had stopped. The father got out and came over to me. I thought he was going to ask for directions to somewhere in the city. To my great surprise, he said, "I see you have a problem with your tyre. I'll fix it for you." Without me even having a chance to say anything he went to the boot of his car and unloaded a full size trolley-jack and within two seconds was jacking up the front of my car. By this time I was outside the car and watching him in total amazement. He had all the tools he needed to remove the wheel, exchange it for the spare wheel in the boot of my car and fit the spare wheel. He then put the trolley-jack back into his car. It took him about three minutes to achieve this. I said you must work in the tyre-fitting trade and he admitted that this used to be his job.

I tried to give him £10 for the work he had done, but he refused. I argued with him and he only and reluctantly accepted the money when I said, "Please buy some ice-creams for your children with this money." He, with his family, cheerfully drove away having performed what I thought was a miracle.

How was it that just at a particular time in a particular place that someone should stop their car and have just the particular tools needed to replace a faulty tyre on another car parked in the same place at the same time?

Pause for thought...

Today be alert and open to whatever life may bring... be fully present to what unfolds and 'see' the light in each person and situation.

Elizabeth Medler

The 'Angel' on the London Underground

This story is one 'coin' with two sides. Sometimes events follow on from each other or come together in order to make a cogent point. In this case the meaning behind two journeys, linked in time by a few days, became quickly apparent.

'Heads'

On 24th December 2014 I had the amazing experience of meeting an 'angel' on the London underground. I was on my way to Hitchin in Hertfordshire to visit my friend, Freya. Christmas was lovely, but one of the best gifts came in the form of the learning experiences derived from the journeys.

I recall that I hadn't felt well and had more or less decided that I would not make the journey to Hitchin. The problem appeared to be a virus which was making me feel dizzy and weak. It seemed hardly possible to negotiate the London underground and find my way to Hitchin. But my friend was encouraging... 'It would be a lovely Christmas and we would go to St Mary's, the Parish Church in Hitchin.' So overcoming my feeling of not wanting to travel, I set off.

Arriving at Victoria Station, I felt distinctly dis-orientated and muzzy headed, 'Was this a good idea?', I asked myself. Normally, I crossed London to Kings Cross and then on to Hitchin without hesitation, but that day I couldn't make sense of anything. Consequently I spoke to a ticket man standing by the entrance to the tube. I asked: 'Can you tell me please which trains I need to take for Kings Cross?' He answered, but I could not seem to retain the information. Just then, out of the blue, a man appeared from nowhere. Much to my surprise, he took my suitcase and said that he had overheard the conversation and that he was going to Kings Cross too. He ushered me towards the moving escalator. I felt extremely vulnerable as I was dis-orientated, but he encouraged me to follow. (I had no choice really as he had my suitcase!) On reaching the bottom of the moving stairs, he said he knew the quickest route through the tunnels to the correct platform for Kings Cross.

The train came promptly and he sat down next to me with my suitcase still firmly in his hands. He was a confident person and said: 'I expect you are wondering who I am?' I said 'yes'. He reached for his pocket and produced an identity card. His name was on it and I believe he was called Andrew Waddell. He said that he worked on the underground and was responsible for switching off the electricity on the train tracks at the end of each day. He indicated that it was an important job as everything had to be powered down in the right order.

Andrew said he was going home to spend time with his children. He asked me where I was going. I prevaricated a bit as I wasn't entirely sure I should divulge my destination, but his direct question seemed to demand a direct response: 'To see friends in Hitchin,' I said. 'Ah', I am going to Hitchin too,' he said. To me, that seemed quite incredible.

We arrived at Kings Cross and he negotiated my suitcase along the platform and up the steps. He knew exactly where he was going and on reaching the station, he knew the time of the next train before we arrived. We clambered on and he put my suitcase in the luggage hold above the seat. He sat near me and indicated that when we arrived, he would take my suitcase down for me. On arrival, that is what he did. I thanked him very much and we said goodbye.

This may seem like a simple story, but the fact was I was not really in a condition to travel and, without Andrew, goodness knows where I might have ended up!

'Tails'

On 27th December, after a wonderful break, I left Hitchin to travel home. However, I was not yet fully recovered and felt quite weak. Getting the train at Hitchin was straightforward, but just before arriving at Finsbury Park where I needed to disembark, the train stopped abruptly and was stationary for nearly an hour. Finally, there was an announcement to the effect that Finsbury Park was closed and would not be reopening for the foreseeable future. We were asked to find alternative routes home. Nobody seemed to know what to do. It was an area of London I didn't know. Some passengers stayed on the train in the hope that it might eventually go somewhere, but most people got off and headed up the stairs for the road. I followed them blindly. However, I was really not sure what to do! I therefore went back to the train and sat for a minute or two. As I sat, there was an announcement to the effect that a train would come in on the other side. I decided to get that on the basis that it might take me to some other station on the underground. Arriving at its destination, I was faced with an unfamiliar setting and wandered along the pavement past a small parade of shops. I asked a young woman in a shop if there was a nearby underground station heading into Victoria, but she couldn't help. Then I asked a man in a restaurant and he gave me directions to Arnos Grove tube. I was not on 'the ball' and wandered around for a while at a loss as to which direction to take. Finally, I found the tube and headed into London and from there, home.

Uniting 'heads' and 'tails'

'Heads' taught me that when we really need help, we receive it, seemingly out of the blue. Andrew Waddell was my angel that day. I was not left unaided, but assisted to reach my destination in every possible way. I felt blessed and supported.

'Tails' taught me that sometimes in life we are left entirely to our own devices. We become lost, but Providence prompts us to rely upon our own mettle and find the way ourselves.

 *Pause for thought...*

Are we alive to the messages written in to our day?

David Beckwith

Changing Direction

David shows how a 'chance' meeting led to a renewal of faith and enrichment of the inner life.

I had left the city and brought my family to the far west of the country and was preparing to start a new life away from the pollution and stress of urban existence.

The unease that I felt had been gradually building for many years before that major decision was made to leave the security of a well paid job and risk everything on a dream that had been ignored for too long.

I had been reasonably successful and had enjoyed my work in civil engineering but it had become apparent that there was a part of me that felt unfulfilled.

My attitude to religion had always been shaped by my connections with the church during my school years. They were spent initially attending a Church of England school where the dogmas of that particular religion were drummed into us on a regular basis.

On Sundays I attended a Free Evangelical Chapel where the teachings seemed at odds with my weekday connections with the school's church.

It was during my teens and early twenties that due to the intransigent teachings of various religions that I moved away from all organised religion. However, I still went to some churches to experience that peace and quietness that can be found within their walls.

Changing Direction

Due to work and family commitments my life had become busy and overcrowded but I always felt that something important was missing. It was this feeling — that gradually became greater — that led me to the decision to change direction.

In our new surroundings with no regular income I relied on what had always been my belief that something would turn up. It had always worked for me in the past so I set about getting work in the area. My first job was to do some decorating. It turned out to be most important as from this I was to meet someone who was to have considerable influence on my life.

I was told that a lady required some work to be carried out at her cottage. I was given the address and asked to call there to assess the work that was needed.

The cottage was tiny and mid-terrace. The door was opened by a small elderly lady and, after I introduced myself, I was invited in. My first impression of the lady and her cottage were that she was very practical and that the cottage was sparsely furnished.

After discussing and agreeing the work to be done she asked me why I had come to live in the area. I explained my circumstances to her and after some time the topic of conversation switched to religious and spiritual awareness. It was the first time that I felt that I could discuss my feelings with anyone and it was with someone who at that time was a stranger.

Amy was a Quaker and had decided to live her life as simply as possible where possessions were concerned. Although in her eighties she was very open minded and interested in art and sciences. Her daily routine started early at about five thirty with exercises and meditation.

Over the next few years I carried out work for Amy but on many occasions we spent far more time discussing theology, books and authors such as Krishnamurti, Tagore and Gibran. Amy also introduced me to the work of Henry Hamblin and *The Science of Thought Review*.

Of all the influences in my life, meeting Amy and my connection with a charity dedicated to raising consciousness — The Hamblin Trust — have been the most life changing.

I had found a new direction in life. I looked at Christianity with clearer eyes, realising that stripped of the dogma, there was a teaching that was compatible with other great religions.

Whether I was destined to meet her, I do not know but I have had experiences in my life when things have happened and there has not been any logical reason behind them so I am open minded on that subject.

I do know that Amy had a very strong faith that carried her through many difficult times and she was always fascinated by rainbows and thought that they were a sign that all was well...

I was away from home when Amy died and news of her passing reached me the following morning. After breakfast I walked out into the countryside and found a place to sit and contemplate. Within a few minutes I looked up and right across the sky was a rainbow of the most brilliant colours.

 *Pause for thought...*

Can we welcome seeming strangers into our lives today?

Terry Parris

God Helps Those Who Help Themselves

In this story a small token reminds Terry of the assistance she received when crossing a busy airport, but an adventure in India prompted her to draw upon her own resources.

'Heads'

A tiny, yellow plastic giraffe on a shelf in my bedroom will always remind me of the 'angel' who accompanied me across Heathrow airport. I had been planning to return to my home in Catalunya after attending a lecture in London. My eldest son, Matthew, took me in a taxi to London's City Airport. We said goodbye and I boarded the plane for Barcelona. After waiting half an hour or so we passengers were told that the plane would not be flying and we must get off, recover our luggage, and get on a bus for a flight from Heathrow.

All this was a bit difficult for me as Heathrow is an enormous airport; I was daunted because I was suffering from a bout of rheumatoid arthritis and had difficulty in walking. With all the other passengers I managed to get out of the bus, collected my pull-along case and a bag full of presents for home, and entered the airport. Almost immediately, a man of about thirty or so, tapped me on the shoulder and spontaneously shouldered my heavy plastic bag and pull-along. Chatting in a friendly manner, we found the gate for departure, after miles of airport corridors. Having an hour to wait, we sat in a café where he ordered drinks, one of which contained a giraffe stirrer for decoration. He refused payment and said he was a policeman and was going to the Costa Brava, where he had a holiday home. Off the plane in Barcelona, he hailed a taxi for me and said goodbye before disappearing. An 'angel' indeed!

'Tails'

My experience in Pune, India, was totally different. I was fifty-four and, prompted by a book written by Bhagwan Shree Rajneesh, I had come out to experience teaching and meditation at his Ashram. I had found my spiritual experiences concurred exactly with Bhagwan's.

In those days there were no credit cards, or at least I didn't have one, and my travellers' cheques had almost run out. I could no longer remain at the Blue Hotel where I was staying. I needed to find cheaper accommodation. My husband had advised me, in case of necessity, to look for the branch of the International Cable Company for which he worked, and stay at their small boarding house, normally used by their Indian employees. So I did this.

I had been exploring the shops in Pune and the torrential Monsoon rain had surprised me. Then darkness suddenly fell as it does in India. I couldn't remember my way back to the boarding house. A group of small Indian children began pelting me with mud and laughing uproariously as I groped my way towards what seemed to be the gatehouse of a great mansion. Light appeared as I shouted out and I glimpsed an Indian security-guard complete with pistols. My explanation of being lost only evoked deep suspicion and no interest. As I moved on, rising panic began to overtake me, but my resistance to it somehow gave me strength. I don't know where it came from. It made me turn back and, in a quiet voice, I repeated the name of the boarding house and asked the guard for directions and a torch. Amazingly, he complied. Somehow, some inner strength that was in me had risen up and taken over. It has never left me.

 *Pause for thought...*

Let's ask for help if we need it today.

Meg Bentley

The Cat on the Bus

Meg's mother passed on a valuable lesson to her daughter — how to live with compassion in the world.

One day we acquired a tabby female kitten. The kitten arrived with an explanation from my mother. It seemed that the kitten had been given to her and she had no choice but to accept! This is what she said:

'A young man sat next to me on the bus. He was crying. I noticed something moving under his sweater and asked if he was alright. His reply astonished me. He told me he had got to take his kitten and get them, the RSPCA, to kill her. A head then squeezed out of the neck of his jumper and a pair of eyes blinked at me. He furiously explained that his mother said it cost too much money to feed; she had enough mouths to feed and had asked him to get rid of it! He had rescued the kitten from some boys who were hurting her and explained that she only needed milk and scraps. He clutched her defensively. I told him 'they' would not put her to sleep but would find her a home, especially as she was so pretty. Suddenly the kitten was thrust onto my lap, the boy jumped up and rushed to get off the bus. I shouted, 'What's your name?' 'Alan' and, 'Yer will won't yer?' I shouted back I would and waved as the bus pulled away. So you see I had to bring her home!'

My mother was never certain he had heard her reply. She kept a photo of the cat in her handbag for years hoping she would see Alan again and tell him that his kitten was fine — it had turned out all right. She settled into our lives becoming my father's constant companion. He called her 'Madam'. She died at the age of twenty-two quietly in her sleep.

Madam's story is shocking in some ways but also expresses compassion, trust and love and a young boy's bravery. Invariably we do not know the true motives of others, but my mother was there and potentially able to soften a deep hurt and bring some healing to the situation. Alan's light shone out because he had rescued his adored friend and then recognised my mother's capacity to understand both his needs and the kitten's. He knew he had found someone who would cherish his little cat.

My mother, who incidentally didn't particularly like cats, acted because of her compassion; she couldn't bear the thought of either Alan or the cat suffering. She also understood the mother's financial worries. She'd experienced difficult times herself but she did not want the boy to remain angry and resentful, hence her acceptance of what turned out to be a clever, very beautiful and loving cat that had a profound effect on all of us.

This account of kindness has affected my attitude to life. Kindness and compassion even when not observed or perhaps not wanted, are fundamental to the way I live. I have not rescued kittens, but I try to remember to smile, start conversations and listen. I don't always remember but my mother's favourite saying sounds in my heart... 'You cannot leave this Earth without making it a better place.'

 *Pause for thought...*

Today, let's welcome the unexpected with kindness and compassion.

Ruth Yendell

The Loving Arms of Providence

When her car broke down in a busy city, Ruth was helped in unexpected ways...

I couldn't understand it... my car was normally so reliable, but with only a small warning rattle at about 7pm on Good Friday, in the centre of town, the clutch went. Had I been at leisure, this would have been something of a challenge, but it was compounded further because I was driving my friend (George) back to his residential home in a nearby village.

Fortunately, Nissan, with whom the car is regularly serviced, had recently supplied me with a 'freebie' combination pack for emergencies, so I put on my hazard lights and went to the boot and dug that out. Eventually I found a luminous triangle which I managed to erect — though not quite correctly — on the road a few yards to the rear of the stationary car. Then I got back into the car and rang my Rescue people. I was just finishing giving all the details when a head appeared at the window — a tall strapping young man — who told me that if I took off the handbrake, he could push me (plus passenger) across the lights to the wide pavement beyond the lights where I would be safer. I hadn't quite finished with the Rescue centre, so was a bit annoyed at first because he seemed to be in a hurry, but eventually I told the emergency people that I would ring them back and off we went. The trouble was, I had switched the engine off, so the steering was locked and with all the shock of it I couldn't think what had happened as we careered dangerously towards a bollard. I eventually realised just in time what had happened, put the brake on briefly, and switched on so that I could use the steering. By the time we had got that sorted, two more young men appeared out of nowhere eager to help.

I was very quickly and efficiently pushed the rest of the way and safely deposited on the wide pavement. Two of the young men vanished before I even had time to thank them, while the first one kindly went back, at my request, to retrieve my 'triangle' before he too disappeared with my thanks ringing in his ears. By this time, another car had pulled in just in front of me and lo and behold a family, whose mother I had known well and been able to help a little, had seen me and stopped to ask if there was anything they could do for me. At first I said, "No, I'm fine, thanks," but then I remembered George, who had been sitting quietly in the passenger seat all this time. I had been wondering how on earth to get him back to the village where his residential home was. My friends, however, live not so far away from his village, so I felt it was reasonable to ask them if they could possibly take him home. They were only too glad to help and completely refused my offer of petrol money. I introduced George, and off they went. Once they'd gone, I sat there for a while on my own, wondering how long it would be before the Rescue chap came, and putting up a few prayers — mostly of gratitude! Then, to my great surprise, the family who had taken George home, reappeared, evidently feeling they should stay with me until help arrived. I was really touched by this and promptly exclaimed, "My guardian angel is working overtime!" These good friends stayed with me until the Rescue man appeared.

It seemed no time at all before a large lorry with a trailer appeared and then I said goodbye to my friends and was left with my next 'angel'. He was greying, stocky in physique, and at first intimidating, not quite what you would expect a real angel to be! However, he immediately and efficiently took command of the situation, ushering me into the lorry cab and deftly parked my car on his trailer. It transpired later that he had been brought up in one of the poorest areas of the city, once famous for crime, and it was to this housing estate, quite nearby, that he drove to find somewhere to turn his now very cumbersome vehicle. He bemoaned the fact that the Council had demolished their little brick church, a small building which I too remembered, and in which his mother and grandmother had been married.

The Council had replaced it with a block of flats. He was deeply indignant that although they promised them another church, it never came.

As it was a Bank Holiday weekend, he felt it was best to take me and the car back to my home until the Tuesday, when I could phone again and get the car taken down to the garage. As we drove back towards my home we exchanged memories of the city as we remembered it so many years ago. It happened that we drove past the extensive Local Government headquarters, and he told me that when he was a kid, the day before Mothering Sunday he and his mates (some thirty of them) used to raid the gardens there for daffodils. I hasten to add that this was because they had no money! They would arrive early in the morning, picking as many as they possibly could until some official turned up to chase them away, and taking armfuls back to their respective mothers. "Not that I approve of thieving," he was quick to say, "I never had the inclination"! Whether the mothers ever knew where they came from, he didn't say.

My road is an extremely narrow one and it took my new 'angel' much concentration to back the trailer up to my home and unload my car. Then he told me what to do on Tuesday to get it down to the garage and we said a friendly, and from me deeply grateful, goodbye.

I was overwhelmed by God's generosity and felt a certain awe at being so well looked after — without in the least bit deserving it!

 *Pause for thought...*

Let's be open to those who come to help us in times of need and express heartfelt thanks.

Part Four

~ Insights ~

'Learn from yesterday, live for today, hope for tomorrow. The important thing is not to stop questioning.'

Albert Einstein

Jane's story
David's story
Jennifer's story
Paul's story
Josephine's story
Rose's story
Michael's story
Jan's story

Jane Pittsinger

How 'El Nino' Synchronously Uprooted my Life and Showed me Compassion

Jane's life changed suddenly when the Pacific Ocean claimed her home.

We had been looking for somewhere to rent for weeks. All rental accommodation within commuting distance to our jobs was filled to capacity. There was one percent availability we were told. In the meantime the constant deluging rain was eating away at the cliff on the edge of the Pacific Ocean and the land at the front of our house was dropping away at an alarming rate.

One morning, I was standing with our next door neighbour on the deck which overlooked the ocean. There was a lull in the rain but we had heard that the tides were to be especially high that day and the next. There was a dull roar as the turbulent, grey sea foamed up to the foot of the cliff. We did not talk much because it was hard to hear our voices. As we stood there — trying not to lean out over the railing to see the rocks and beach some sixty feet below — I caught a movement out of the corner of my eye to our right. The far end of the deck was bending down in slow motion. My neighbour, Joe, saw it too and we stepped back to the left, and then stepped back again and again as the deck peeled away towards us. When we stood on his land, we saw the entire deck fall silently away and plunge to the beach below. There was no sound because of the crashing waves.

The house itself now stood flush with the precipice of the cliff and most probably the foundations were undercut. My husband was in the bedroom at the edge of the cliff, not aware of what had transpired. Someone contacted the fire department. Subsequently, yellow tape was strung all around the house and evacuation was ordered. Fortunately we had moved my fragile father-in-law to his youngest son's tiny one room 'studio' apartment the week before. We had also taken a week off work in order to begin packing up our belongings and to move away from the cliff edge of the house — just in case. The timing was, in fact, quite good! From another perspective the timing was not good at all... Not only were my parents due to visit from England in two weeks, but my brother-in-law and his wife from the Czech Republic, were intending to start a new life with us soon after my parents had left. We had nowhere to live. I redoubled my search for accommodation.

I rang my friend who had offered to store some of our belongings in her small shed. She asked me why I was ringing so early in the morning. When I told her, she said: "You are coming here to live with us." She organized her mother and father to bring a pick-up truck and asked her neighbour if we might use her garage for furniture storage. After that, she came and picked up our disoriented cat and then set to packing up every last item we owned. Passers-by who had come to view the falling cliff (filmed by helicopters and circulating TV vans) went to get boxes from the local store; other people just pitched in, a passing preacher offered his prayers. Someone across the street rigged up fluorescent lights so that we could see after dark to pack up our last belongings. It was forbidden by law to re-enter the house and garage once we had left.

That night the rain returned in spades but we slept well for the first time in months, waking up to know that the hillside was not sliding from under us. The cat gently snored at the foot of our bed.

The next day I resumed the search for accommodation while my husband went to work. I made many phone calls, and visited every apartment building I could think of. Strangely, I came across an apartment complex called 'Land's End'. Desiree, the property manager, whose name I shall not forget, told me that they had nothing available in the foreseeable future, especially since some of their empty flats had been flooded. I went to work that afternoon, despondent. When I arrived, the receptionist told me that someone called Desiree had called. I rang back. She told me that right after I left her office a couple came in and said that they needed to leave in two weeks' time. It was a two bedroom apartment. Would we like it?

We moved in just in time for the arrival of my brother-in-law and his wife who now had their own bedroom. At the same time a place opened up on a waiting list for an assisted living centre for my father-in-law. So much happened in the next few months. It seemed to me that one thing led into the next in an ordered process. A cousin in San Francisco died and, knowing well our predicament, left us a legacy as a down payment on a house. My husband, myself and in-laws all moved in and benefitted from my brother-in-law's real estate experience. My father-in-law died but his three sons were all with him. Countless people offered to help us and to have us stay with them in their homes. We could no longer watch the dolphins and whales from our sitting room but we could rest easily at night and walk to the ocean in the morning.

I learned to know deeply that I was not in control. As we came to each step and its unfoldment I knew that I could trust that all would be well. As my friend says: "It is nice to have that in your pocket". It is in my pocket, the one over my heart, and when I am uncertain about the future I remember this experience and how, despite its many challenges, I could rest back and trust the support of people and the universe at large. I came to know and to trust the compassion of human beings.

 *Pause for thought...*

Can you extend a helping hand today to a friend or stranger in need?

David Millican

A Premonition or Just a Dream?

David's dream of a premature death and subsequent Tarot card reading led him to explore his inner life through meditation. This pierced the veil of the material world and he was able to glimpse something of the beauty of infinity.

Many years ago, while sleeping, I became aware that I was having a lucid dream — I was dreaming, but at the same time I was aware I was dreaming. In the dream, I was walking along a busy pavement in an unknown town. Realising it was a dream, I decided to try and change it. I began by greeting the people walking towards me, and to my great joy, they each responded by smiling and greeting me in return. Emboldened by that, I decided to try something more adventurous, and stepped into the air and began to fly. I climbed high into the sky, and flew firstly over the town, and then over the hills, fields, and rivers surrounding it. Shortly, I noticed a cemetery on the summit of a hill in the distance and decided to take a closer look. I slowly descended towards it, feeling strangely drawn towards a particular gravestone. Upon approaching it, I saw to my horror that it had my name on it, along with the inscription 'died aged 23'. I woke up with a start. I was twenty-two at the time.

For some time after that night, I felt deeply disturbed by the experience, and one day decided to seek the help of a friend. She was known by many as a wise and sensitive soul, and gifted at reading the Tarot cards. We met at her home, and I asked her to read the cards for me. I mentioned that I had a specific question in mind but did not give her any details. After the cards had been spread in a particular pattern, she turned over the first two cards, explaining that they represented the questioner and the question. They were the two and three of the same suit. I no longer remember which suit, or much else about the rest of the reading, as my mind was by then in a spin. However, I do remember the final card, which I was told represented the likely outcome and answer to my question; it was the Death card. A few weeks later I turned twenty-three.

For much of my life prior to that time, I had been confused — even depressed — about where my life was leading. There was no meaning or purpose to it; I was just drifting along mindlessly, but now, prompted by the dream and the Tarot reading, I started to reflect more on life and search for a purpose. I moved to the countryside to live on my own, and to get more time and space to think. I read numerous books on different religions and philosophies, and tried to teach myself to meditate, but could find no answers anywhere. Then, one day I heard that there was to be an introductory talk on Transcendental Meditation (TM) to be held nearby, so I went along to find out more. The talk was relatively interesting, and the speaker inspiring, and so I signed up to be taught the technique the following week.

When the day came, I went along to a private house in the next village to where I was staying, and after a short ceremony, was given my mantra. What happened next was unlike anything I had experienced before. The moment I began to meditate, I felt my mind and body drop dramatically into a state of deep relaxation, and intense feelings of warmth and love washed over me. What followed, is mostly indescribable: my mind seemed to expand to infinity, all sensations of time and space disappeared, and an astonishingly beautiful and peaceful realm hidden behind the mundane world was revealed. It was as though a door had been opened in my mind that up until then had been firmly closed, but just waiting for the right time to be opened.

When the teacher indicated it was time to stop meditating, I found myself unable to speak. The world seemed different, somehow refreshed, and I felt changed. I left the house and walked the two miles home, holding a flower in front of me that the teacher had given me, feeling as though my whole self was beaming at the sheer joy of being alive.

A Premonition or Just a Dream?

Over time, most of the effects faded, but they left their mark. I soon realised that the experience had changed me in a very profound way: I now knew for certain that there was something infinitely beautiful and good hidden behind the material world we live in, and that I had been blessed with just a tiny glimpse of it. I also knew that what I wanted now, more than anything else in life, was to seek out that realm again and to deepen my understanding of it. I had found my purpose in life.

When I look back over the forty or so years since that experience, I can see many changes in my life that have a single connecting thread running through them: other meditation techniques have been learnt and practised, different religious and philosophical groups have been joined, books have been read, and ideas explored, but they have all been done in the further pursuit of what I had first glimpsed so many years before.

I have no way of knowing whether the lucid dream I had was a premonition or not, or whether the Tarot reading was simply a coincidence; however, I do know that together they encouraged me to seek out answers to life's important questions, and this led to an experience which dramatically changed my life. I also know that, as predicted in the dream and the Tarot reading, a significant part of my old life died when I was twenty-three, and a new life began, and for that, I will be forever grateful.

 *Pause for thought...*

Allow your mind and body to drop into a state of deep relaxation. Repeat some words you find soothing and inspirational and allow the curtain of the physical to lift...

Jennifer Dunkley

Mrs Emsley and the Tea Leaves

Mrs Emsley's gift of seeing into the future poses questions for us all… does the future exist before it happens?

Years ago my husband, Chris, received a compulsory transfer to work in East London. This was not our wish at all. He started his commute, staying in London all week, leaving me and our new baby behind.

Not long after this we took a short holiday in Yorkshire to stay with Chris' parents. My mother-in-law invited a friend round for a 'cuppa'. Thelma Emsley read tea leaves but only for friends. She offered to read ours. Her advice was not to spend any money redecorating as she 'saw' that we would be moving to a new abode next to a field of horses. There were white gable ends on the house and gulls flying around.

Commuting was tiring for Chris and he missed us greatly in his rather limited one-room digs. We decided that we would have to move. We house hunted in Chelmsford and paid a deposit for a bog-standard semi on a large estate. It was all we could afford. There was no field, horses or gulls. Mrs Emsley was clearly wrong about her predictions this time.

Chris had already requested a transfer back to Dover, but this seemed distinctly unlikely. A few weeks later he was advised that his transfer request had been granted and he would be moved back within a few months. However, we had paid a sizeable deposit on our chosen property. What should we do? Our stress levels peaked! Soon after this, we had our deposit returned. We had been 'gazumped', meaning that although our offer had been accepted, someone had made a higher offer and that had been accepted instead. In our case though it was a joy and relief! However, Mrs Emsley was wrong again as our little two-bed bungalow wasn't next to a field.

We forgot all about Mrs Emsley and moving for another year or so. Then daughter number two came along and we decided that we must look for a larger property in the lovely village where we had our roots. I went for a walk with our two offspring and at the edge of the village I saw two new properties being erected. The foreman showed me the plans. The building had just started. A friend of ours was living in an almost identical bungalow elsewhere in the village so we knew how it would look eventually. We again placed our deposit for it. We got to know the builders and sub-contractors who allowed us to choose our colours, plug points and interiors. We were so happy... and what is more, it was next to a field of horses and a mile from the sea. It was within our grasp. Then came another 'bombshell' — another couple were willing to pay more than the asking price for the bungalow. Our hopes were dashed. Mrs Emsley had got it wrong yet again!

A few days later, the builder phoned us, and feeling sorry for our disappointment turned down the other couple's higher offer.

Mrs Emsley was right and what is more, she 'saw' our new bungalow before it had even been built.

Pause for thought...

Can we let go of all expectation and trust that what is right and good will unfold...

Paul A Janke

My Epiphany

Paul's life was in pieces, but his enjoyment of Nature and an afternoon walk brought unexpected renewal and hope.

My world, as I knew it, was ending! How would I cope? What was I going to do next? I had just been made redundant from my post as Financial Accountant at an electronics engineering company. I couldn't quite understand why I felt so devastated and despairing. After all, I was looking to change my career, anyway. I was already half way through a four-year part-time course in homoeopathy. But, that was part of the problem — how would I afford to live, let alone pay for the final two years of the course? Everything seemed so dark and hopeless.

After several weeks of introspection I started to understand why I was feeling the way I did. Despite the fact that I loathed my role as an accountant, it had become a major part of my personal identity. Like so many other people, I had come to define myself by my job — and now it was gone! I felt totally unwanted, worthless and useless. I even became somewhat agoraphobic — frightened to go out in the daytime when I should be at work, in case people saw me and judged me as being lazy or a skiver. I had been raised with a very strong work ethic and struggled with the fact I was at home all day while my wife had to go out and bring home the bacon.

All in all, I felt pretty much destroyed by being rejected (as I saw it) by a company I had given excellent service to for many years. This destruction of my ego was made worse when I had to 'sign on' the dole and was obliged to attend Job Club each week day.

Over the course of the next couple of months I applied for hundreds of jobs. However, I did not receive the courtesy of a single reply. Bearing in mind that I was an experienced accountant with twenty years under my belt, including some prestigious positions, reinforced the feeling of no longer being wanted. Privately I wondered if I was 'over the hill'. My confidence was so shaken that, in the end, I couldn't stand the rejection and I signed myself off the dole.

I was at the lowest ebb of my life. It was then that I discovered that one of the few things that would provide me with a modicum of succour was being in Nature. Fortunately, the modern housing estate on which I lived was bordered by a nature reserve, so I used to force myself to overcome my agoraphobic tendencies and go walking in the woods. It was during one of these excursions that I had an epiphany! That particular day I was feeling so low and utterly worthless, I paused to sit down on a tree stump next to the stream to have a weep. As the tears flowed, I heard a voice in my head. This came as a bit of a surprise, to say the least, as I was in no way religious and having long since rejected my Christian upbringing. Nevertheless, the dialogue went something like this:

Voice: "Why the tears?"

Me: "I have lost my job. I don't know how to do anything else. My relationship is suffering. Money is running out. Nobody wants me. I am at the end of my tether. I feel useless. I am totally worthless. I don't see the point of going on."

Voice: "I understand why you feel that way but that doesn't make it true."

Me: "What do you mean?"

Voice: "Do you like where you are sitting, now?"

Me: "Yes, it is beautiful."

Voice: "Do you like the trees all around you and the stream flowing next to you?"

Me: "Yes."

Voice: "Do you like the birdsong all around you?"

Me: "Yes."

Voice: "Do you like the scent of the blossom and the earthy smell of the damp ground?"

Me: "Yes."

Voice: "Do you love your pet cats waiting for you back at your home?"

Me: "Yes."

Voice: "Do you enjoy your trips to the coast and swimming in the sea?"

Me (becoming slightly exasperated at this line of questioning): "Yes — please get to the point!"

Voice: "I am getting there. Who do you think created all these things that you appreciate, love and enjoy so much?"

Me: "I never thought I would hear myself saying such a thing, but You, I suppose."

Voice: "Who do you think created you and all of humanity?"

Me: "You, I suppose."

Voice: "And do you think I would put any less effort into creating you than I did into creating the natural world that you love so much; especially as I have given you and your kind stewardship of it all? How can you be worth less than that which you are here to nurture and care for?"

I couldn't fault this logic and it all suddenly became clear to me... I was part of this amazing creation called 'life' and I was no greater or smaller than any part of it. Ever since that epiphany, much of my time has been spent in helping people rediscover their innate worthiness. My own sense of worth is enhanced by helping others to find theirs.

 *Pause for thought...*

Take a moment of your day to relish Nature. Pause and enjoy the lulling breezes, the rain or the warm sun on your cheek. Listen...

Josephine Chia

Chant Your Way Out of Distress

Josephine shows how we can rise above our difficulties and gain valuable insights by chanting to ourselves meaningful words and texts.

This story has a happy ending.

I want to share it with you so that you too can feel empowered. Sometimes when we are going through difficult life challenges, we don't think that we can come out on the other side. Now that I am out of the difficulties I was in, I can assure you that there are always unseen beings of light to help us. But we need to be able to access that help. Mine came through chanting.

The last fifteen years of my life have seen some of the greatest challenges I have had to face. My family are Peranakans, a combination of Chinese ancestry and Malay language and customs. I believe we are the true Singaporeans. I was brought up in what was a section of a cow shed with no running water or electricity. My mother delivered me alone with no midwife to assist her. Despite the poverty all around me, I was encouraged to be resourceful. I always had a keen desire to educate myself and I later became an Assistant Dental Nurse and read for a Masters in Creative Writing at Bath Spa University. Before all this, I married in my native land but was soon divorced. However, some decades later, I fell in love again, this time to David, an Englishman. We were married and I came to live in England. The marriage was to last for twenty years. The toughest decision I made was to leave David — a man I felt I still loved. Deep down I knew I had to do so for my safety and my sanity.

Chant Your Way Out of Distress

For a middle-aged Asian woman to get divorced once was bad enough, but to get divorced for a second time was a social disaster. I felt like an absolute failure. I knew that there would be many stones that would be hurled at me, so I was reluctant to make the decision.

I encouraged my husband seek psychiatric help. I was willing to go with him and be subjected to medical scrutiny in case any of his problems were due to me. He usually blamed me for his anger. Heavy drinking had morphed him into an abusive bully, verbally, mentally and, eventually, physically. I made excuses to friends about my bruised eyes, split lips and damaged eardrum. After a visit to an eminent psychologist in Harley Street, my husband claimed he was not the problem and that I was. That was when I knew I had to leave him. One can only accept so much blame.

It was only after I left that I realised how toxic the relationship was. I had to fit in to his image of an Asian wife. Thinking back to my first divorce, I came to see that my driving need was to be loved and that this had blinded me in my choice of partners. After the divorce, I was in much reduced circumstances and all alone in a foreign land.

It was not long after that I saw a film about Tina Turner who also suffered at the hands of an abusive husband. She found excuses not to leave. A friend introduced her to a mantra, *Namyoho Renge Kyo*, which I discovered later was from Japanese Daishonin Buddhism. I went to a group that taught the chant and was encouraged by its efficacy.

In my utter feeling of hopelessness and distress, I stepped up on my yoga and spiritual practices; studied with many world famous spiritual leaders and gurus, the Dalai Lama, Thich Nhat Hanh, Eckhart Tolle, Wayne Dyer and many others. Through the teachings of Sufi Master, Hazrat Inayat Khan, Thomas Ashley Ferrand and others, I learnt more about the power of mantras.

The proper use of mantras works like a tuning fork that increases the vibrations within your energy body. When we are in distress or egoistic pursuits, our attention is focussed on our physical self, thus making us lose sight of our true nature. When our vibration is higher, we enter awareness and become conscious of who we really are. The peace and strength that comes with the awakening of our spiritual Self gives us clarity so we can deal with all our problems in a different way. Amazingly, solutions to our problems also appear. You don't have to accept the belief that mantras have power, just experience them yourself to find out the truth. I did and it transformed my life.

Pause for thought...

Find some inspiring text which is meaningful to you and gently chant the lines at odd moments throughout the day.

Rose McCray

My Hip Journey

Rose's journey reveals important lessons about humility and faith. Do we have the humility to modify our deeply entrenched views and trust the process?

The lights blazed behind double doors across the carpeted landing. I fought against a desire to run, pulled my gown around me and followed the assistant through to theatre. My surgeon stood in a corner with his arms crossed, legs apart, looking more like a prize fighter waiting for his opponent than a highly skilled, clinical operator. His eyes were cool and he did not speak. Ready for action.

When I woke eighty minutes later, in recovery, I felt deliciously sleepy, pain-free and glad to be alive. I had survived. The following few days passed in a blur of painkillers, nausea, meals, visits, trying to walk on crutches and, finally, I was at home, with plenty of time to think about my 'hip journey'.

Like a lot of people, probably, I had assumed I would retain total health and strength into my 60s, 70s and possibly into my 80s, even if occasionally infected by colds and other common maladies. I take care with diet and most days I cook fresh meals. I enjoy walking, Pilates and Yoga. As a complementary therapist, I have for a long time advised clients on healthy lifestyle and dietary changes. I have always subscribed to the view that we bring ill health on ourselves by allowing our bodies and minds to get out of kilter. My view has always been that people need to keep out of the hands of doctors who would rather prescribe painkillers than look for the cause of illness. I could hear my own disapproval when responding to clients who saw their doctors on a regular basis rather than looking within for the causes of disease.

Approaching menopause quite late, at 57, I began to find some difficulty in walking, with groin pain — a classic symptom of a hip problem — though I was not aware of that at the time. From then on, I saw my own doctor probably twice a year, had X-rays and bone density testing and appointments to discuss my problem. I had joined the 'system' and was unhappy about it but there seemed to be no other way. I had looked at diet and exercise again, and discovered that an acid-free diet might help me, yet I found it oddly difficult to change my habits. It seemed I had succumbed to osteoarthritis. Me? Impossible! Worse, my lumbar spine showed osteopoenia, the precursor of osteoporosis.

Osteopaths and chiropractors kept me going for eight years, along with a wonderful dog. He was my first ever dog and he made me walk twice daily. Magically, as I walked, the pain eventually almost disappeared during the day, though it returned at night. Then my dog died.

No longer having to walk, I slowed to a full stop. My doctor reviewed the results of tests and recommended, again, painkillers and the customary course of bisphosphonates for osteoporosis. I rejected his advice and chose a new doctor in my own village, for a second opinion. Combined with a grudging acceptance that I needed external help, I knew that I had to insist on a visit to a consultant. My first visit, I decided, was going to be difficult. My new doctor looked at the sore knee I presented him with, then checked my notes and saw the hip X-rays. Immediately, he offered to refer me on a fast-track system to the local Spire hospital, paid for by the NHS, to see a consultant with a view to hip replacement — if necessary. I saw my consultant within two weeks and had a new hip within three months. There had been no need to gird myself up for a confrontation.

From an entrenched position of total antipathy to doctors, with what I saw as their total reliance on drug therapy, I realise that my reaction was one of denial. I lacked, too, a proper appreciation of how I could be helped by the skills and training of the right practitioner. My lack of trust revealed a lack of faith that the outcome would be the best thing that could happen. In all other areas of my life I have adopted a position of trust, that as long as I don't worry, things really do work out for the best — by angelic intervention, serendipity or whatever. But when it had come to my personal health, my own body, I could not accept interference, as I saw it. Until, that is, I could bear the pain no longer and decided to trust the process fully. Then all the balls lined up and fell smoothly into place, to my complete astonishment.

Looking at my situation and my feelings in retrospect, I can see that by virtue of free will I was 'encouraged' to take the first step, to make that initial decision to see a new doctor. I expected to fight for treatment, yet I was offered it. I anticipated a difficult interview with the surgeon, yet it was pleasant and informative. It was made very clear that the surgical choice was mine to make — it would not be forced on me in any way. On the contrary, I was required to be quite certain it was what I wanted. Everyone, from pre-operative assessment nurse to Joint School to ward staff, was helpful, agreeable and encouraging.

The words of my mother ring in my ears at this point: 'You always know best! You are always right!' I disagreed with her at the time, saying that I was often wrong and I was only too aware of it. I was also ready to apologise if I was wrong, so how could I possibly be accused of 'always thinking I knew best'? Fundamentally, though, I think she is right. I nearly always believe I have the answer to my own problems, at least, if I can just work out how to reach it. In this case, I was definitely guided to the solution I needed by being ready to reach out and accept help from people better qualified than myself.

In a sense, this has been a humbling experience. In another sense, I see it as a lesson I needed to learn. Arrogance could have prevented me from seeking help at a time when I most needed it, yet the pieces of the puzzle moved into position almost without any assistance from me. I have not been able to offer treatments to others for some time and have slightly lost touch with my Reiki foundation. Perhaps this experience came to remind me that, in a crisis, we have only to hand over the reins to a greater power that cares for each and every one of us, and have faith in the outcome.

Pause for thought...

Can you identify an area of your life where you are 'digging in your heels'? Do you have the courage to soften and open to another perspective?

Michael Lewin

Questions and Answers —
Sitting and Waiting Respectfully

Michael throws down a gauntlet for us all... can we 'sit' with our questions and listen patiently for the 'still small voice' when it comes?

There is a Jewish fable about an inquisitive man who wanted to seek an answer to a particular question that was bothering him greatly. He had wrestled with this question for many years but had found no real solution, no real answer, so he decided to seek out the wisdom of a famous Hasidic teacher.

He embarked on his journey with enthusiasm and commitment thinking that he would find, at last, some kind of resolution from the wise master. Days were spent walking and resting until he finally reached his destination. Unfortunately the master's assistant told him that it wasn't possible to see him straight away. The assistant pondered... how could the man's question warrant an answer so soon after his arrival? Surely the master would not wish to be disturbed, engaged as he would be in profound philosophical issues. Surely this man's question could wait? Finally, after many days of waiting to see the master the man reached the end of his tether and entered the master's study to confront him, exploding with his question: *'What is the essence of truth?'* The master looked directly into the man's eyes and, surprisingly, slapped him in the face. Outraged the man left and sought refuge in the local inn to bemoan his fate to anyone who would listen. Soon after the assistant arrived in the tavern and explained to the man that the master had hit him not out of any animosity but rather out of reverence. He was trying to say: *'Never surrender a good question for a mere answer!'*

In earlier years, with an inquisitive mind and unbounded impatience, I often asked questions that seemed to require concise answers. After all, I thought, the answers are 'out there' somewhere — laid out in a rational, objective manner — surely I was deserving enough to discover the truth? Now, looking back, I can see how naïve and imprudent I was in attempting to push for closure in terms of finding immediate answers to my questions. Much later a friend said to me: *'A conclusion is a place where you stop thinking.'* This really resonated with me at that time and I never forgot it.

With age my perspective has shifted and changed quite dramatically. I am increasingly brought into a space of 'not knowing' which I'm happy now to occupy, waiting patiently to see if some response will appear, or not. Sitting and waiting reverentially, I now know that 'answers' as we know them may not appear, but invariably there is a deepening of the questions and a gratitude for simply being present to ask them. Like many of you, I have found that questions are often 'answered' in ways we least expect.

Pause for thought...

Today, frame a question clearly and succinctly — feel the import of it throughout your whole being — then firmly, let it go. Refrain from mulling it over. Be open to whatever comes...

Jan Walker

Awakening to my Creative Heart

Jan lives in a town called Paradise in California. Her life was turned upside down when she was obliged to leave the job she loved, but a new and better life emerged.

I could hear my boss shouting from outside in the hospital car park when I arrived for work one day. *'She-Who-Whispers-When-She's-Angry'* had lost it! What on earth could be happening? No one would meet my gaze when I entered the Human Resources building. It was a moment that would change my life completely.

I made my way to my office in Employee Health at the end of the hall. The shouting stopped. The door of our new Director's office opened and I was invited to enter. Our new boss informed me that I was being made redundant. After seven years in Human Resources I would be the first to go under a new regime; new management that would cut the workforce of many of its senior employees. They would follow the usual pattern of dismissing the employees with larger salaries and replacing us with new, younger ones at much reduced cost. My job as Workers Compensation Coordinator would be eliminated.

Our team had improved safety measures around the hospital and provided support to employees in all departments. It had been a joy to serve the community in this way. We were not the usual 'injury police', but had enjoyed improving relationships and infrastructure to benefit everyone. So, as I cleared out my desk and got ready to go for the last time, feeling rather stunned, I couldn't imagine life without my little country hospital. What was I to do?

I went home and sat in shock for a bit, and spent too much time seething with helpless fury. But, I reasoned, this shock with its accompanying fears could not be allowed to wreck my whole life. I looked at my list of talents and skills and in twenty-first century terms, I felt I was still very much in my prime at sixty-two. I firmly believed I would have another job before a month was out. Unfortunately, it was the last years of the economic recession in the United States and I would find that there were no jobs, and plenty more like me competing for those that came along. This was the biggest shock of all.

It was hard not to despair but being by nature an optimist, I sent out many applications and résumés. It was some time before the hard facts hit me and I realized that there would be no new employment for me of the kind I was used to. To cheer myself up, I began to teach Chinese painting classes at my local Recreation Department. This saved me, and as I settled into my new life I began to wake up into my creative heart that I had abandoned long ago.

I joined the local Paradise Art Center, taught classes in Chinese brush painting there, and expanded my teaching into the larger town down the mountain. I began to take classes in arts that I hadn't tried before, or hadn't done in years. As I made new friends and explored my creative side, something miraculous began to happen. I realized one day that I was at long last living my true life — time to paint, learn new things, make artist friends, show and share my true passion in life.

I also began, at last, to write again. My re-awakening into a joyful and creative life took off. I realized that losing the life I believed I needed and embarking on a new adventure, had given me back friendships, both spiritual and artistic, and the rich creativity I so relished.

 *Pause for thought...*

Today let us embrace change and prepare to be transformed!

I would suggest that you brew yourselves a nice cup of tea, make yourself comfortable and enjoy the experience. I found these short stories delightful and they certainly inspired me. So much so that I was lulled into reminiscing on the stories in my own life which I might be tempted to share. It also got me wondering how many other 'short stories' are out there of similar charming and enjoyable tales. I so much recommend this enchanting book but only on the premise that you allow yourselves time to sit back and relax.

Astra Ferro
www.astrajuliaferro.com

A perfect read for the busy, stressful times in which we live. This book urges us to savour, value and be thankful for whatever we encounter in life. It encourages us to be perceptive in interpreting hidden meanings behind events and 'chance' meetings and receptive, open-minded and trusting in life's wisdom.

Through the experiences shared in these stories, and the wise words offered in each of the 'pause' points, this inspiring book helps us to live well in today's challenging world and in charting our passage on this planet.

It conveys a comforting message: that despite experiences to the contrary, everything is unfolding perfectly for our highest good. We see (often with hindsight) that at every point we are looked after. All is well, even though it is not always evident or seems so initially.

Debbie Sellwood
www.debbiesellwood.com

What a treasure trove of delightful short stories Liz Medler has collated. From Guardian Angels to a cat on a bus, these are tales to delight and inspire. Each story is followed by a short pause, to use the insights garnered. A cornucopia indeed.

Murray Morison — Author of Time Sphere
www.wandererchronicle.com